Bluebell Railway Recollections
2nd edition

Contents

Acknowledgments

I would like to thank the many photographers who, once again, have generously allowed me to use their work in the second edition of this book. Without their presence to witness events at the railway, both momentous and day-to-day, this volume would have been immeasurably the poorer. I should also apologise to all those who no doubt have photographs much better than those of mine that I have included, for not looking more widely for contributions; I plead lack of time and also an innate dislike of making difficult decisions, which would have been even more necessary with a wider range of images from which to choose. I also want to thank Nikki Favell for her support with the project. Above all, I want to thank the many people who give so freely of their spare time to volunteer at the railway. Without them, the story that is told in this book would have ended many years ago.

Keith Leppard

About the author

Keith Leppard has been a life-long steam enthusiast with a particular passion for the Bluebell Railway. It was his local preserved railway during his childhood and he began volunteering there in the fledgling Carriage & Wagon Department in 1970. This early involvement with carriage restoration sparked his interest in the craftsmanship and engineering found in carriages of the steam era. While work later took him away from the area and from active volunteering he remained a very engaged 'armchair' member of the Bluebell Railway Preservation Society, writing the first edition of this book in 2013 to coincide with the railway reopening to East Grinstead. He has recently begun to volunteer at the railway again, still focusing on the railway's vintage carriages.

Front cover: **BLUEBELL IN WINTER** A crisp winter's day in December 2017 sees British Railways Standard Class 5 No 73082 *Camelot* catch the low afternoon sun as it speeds northbound past Three Arch Bridge towards Horsted Keynes with a six-coach 'Santa Special'. *Dave Bowles*

Frontispiece: **BLUEBELL IN AUTUMN** LBSCR Class 'A1' No 672 *Fenchurch* completes the autumn scene in November 2006 as it heads a train of Victorian carriages south past Tremains, between Horsted Keynes and Sheffield Park. This was a 'top and tail' service; sister engine No 55 *Stepney* is assisting on the rear of the train. *Jon Bowers*

First published in 2013
Revised and extended 2nd edition first published 2021

British Library Cataloguing in Publication Data

A catalogue record for this book is available from the British Library.

Printed and bound in the Czech Republic

Silver Link Books
Mortons Media Group Limited
Media Centre
Morton Way
Horncastle
LN9 6JR
Tel/Fax: 01507 529535

email: sohara@mortons.co.uk
Website: www.nostalgiacollection.com

1959 a small band of enthusiasts, foreseeing the end of steam power on Britain's railways, came together 'to preserve the puffer for posterity'. Their focus was a recently closed route that ran northwards from the Sussex coast at Lewes through the Ouse valley and the Sussex Weald to the town East Grinstead. Having first hoped to reopen the entire line, practicalities forced them to settle for operating a 5-mile stretch from Sheffield Park to Horsted Keynes. The Bluebell Railway began public services over this route on 7 August 1960, becoming the first standard-gauge preserved passenger line in the country. From those beginnings, a major part of the Bluebell story from the mid-1970s concerned its efforts to reopen the route north to reconnect with the main railway network. These efforts culminated March 2013 with the return of steam trains to East Grinstead.

The future Bluebell Railway route began life with incorporation of the Lewis & East Grinstead Railway by Act of Parliament in 1877. This company amalgamated with the main railway operator in the area, the London, Brighton & South Coast Railway (LBSCR), in 1878, which then built the line. It opened on 1 August 1882 serving stations at Barcombe, Newick & Chailey, Sheffield Park, Horsted Keynes, West Hoathly and Kingscote. A branch from Horsted Keynes westwards to the LBSCR main line Haywards Heath was opened in September 1883 with an intermediate station at Ardingly.

The line was provided with lavish, ornate stations, and the earthworks, bridges and tunnels were built for double track, though only East Grinstead to Haywards Heath was ever laid as such. All the stations had sidings and facilities for handling goods as it was hoped there would be substantial freight traffic, and milk was indeed a major source of revenue for many years. The prospects still looked bright when the branch from Haywards Heath to Horsted Keynes was electrified in 1935; there were post-war plans to extend this northwards to East Grinstead, but these never materialised.

In fact, traffic on the future Bluebell line had already dwindled in the face of competition from road haulage, leading to its first closure in 1955. However Miss Bessemer, a local resident, protested that the 1877 Act required a certain number of passenger trains to be run, so some services had to be reinstated while the Act was repealed; final closure took place on 16 March 1958. Miss Bessemer's intervention proved invaluable in the formation of the Bluebell Railway. Without her it is unlikely that the closure of a sleepy Sussex branch line would have come to wide public attention and the enthusiast flame might never have been lit. Now celebrating its 60th anniversary in 2020, the Bluebell Railway is a large and thriving enterprise.

Being so early in the field of railway preservation, the Bluebell was able to acquire many historic steam locomotives, carriages and wagons, often directly from service with British Railways. With other owner societies coming subsequently to join the Bluebell community with their prized possessions, the railway is now home to a magnificent collection that dates back to the 1860s, mostly from the railway companies that operated in southern England. The Bluebell aims to run regular service trains that reflect the different eras in its collection, so visitors often have the chance to experience trains that are more than 100 years old.

This book brings you this Bluebell journey – both along the line and through its first 60 years – in pictures. Enjoy the ride!

BERNARD HOLDEN MBE The Bluebell Railway Preservation Society's late president, Bernard Holden (seated) at East Grinstead station's formal opening in September 2010, flanked by senior members of the Society. Bernard chaired the inaugural meeting of the Society in 1959 and worked with and for the Bluebell Railway throughout its first 50 years. He passed away in October 2012, sadly just missing the chance to ride on the first Bluebell steam train to East Grinstead. Without him it is hard to imagine that the railway would have survived and flourished as it has. *Derek Hayward*

Bluebell Beginnings

Right: **THE VERY BEGINNING!** After the initial meetings and discussions, the first Bluebell rolling stock arrived at the railway on 17 May 1960. Southern Railway Brake Composite No 6575, built in 1929, and London & South Western Railway (LSWR) non-corridor Lavatory 3rd No 320, built in 1900, were headed by LBSCR 'A1X' No 55, formerly named *Stepney*. They came over the still operational Ardingly branch and are seen here heading south out of Horsted Keynes onto Bluebell metals for the first time.
Bluebell Railway Archive (J. L. Smith)

Below: **PREPARING FOR THE PUBLIC** A lot needed to be done to get ready for the first Bluebell Railway passenger service. Much as happens when a business changes ownership today, corporate branding was not neglected. The engines were left in black livery, but were re-lined and prominently named on the tanks, whilst the coaches were transformed into Bluebell blue livery. Here, the railway's second locomotive, South Eastern & Chatham Railway (SECR) Class 'P' No 323 *Bluebell*, poses with coach 320 in July 1960 while work continues on the second vehicle, No 6575. *Ron Fisher*

Below right: **BLUEBELL HALT** During the 1960/61 seasons, public trains were only allowed as far north as Bluebell Halt, a temporary wooden platform located a short distance south of the junction at Horsted Keynes station. Trains only began running into Horsted Keynes station – still shared with the British Railways service on the Ardingly branch – or 29 October 1961, the last day of the season. *Bluebell Archive*

Right: **FIRST PUBLIC SERVICE** LBSCR 'A1X' No 55, now with its name restored to its side tanks, is the centre of attention for crowds at Sheffield Park on August 1960, the day the railway opened to the public. *Ron Fisher*

Below: **EARLY ARRIVALS** SECR 'P' Class No 27 arrived at the railway in the spring of 1961 and was immediately christened *Primrose* to match its sister engine No 323 *Bluebell*. However, for the 1963 season No 27 was repainted into lined SECR passenger livery, losing its name in the process, and ran in this guise until the mid-1970s. It is seen here with the railway's two SECR carriages on a southbound service of that period. Repairs to No 27 were started in the 1980s but proved too complex, so the engine was set aside as a kit of parts, work only recommencing in 2012. *Bluebell Archive (David Christie)*

Below right: **EARLY ARRIVALS** The LBSCR ancestry of the Bluebell line meant that in its early days the railway was keen to obtain LBSCR locomotives. But after No 55 *Stepney*, it had to wait until October 1962 for the arrival of LBSCR Class 'E4' No 473 *Birch Grove* – the sixth locomotive acquired. Built in 1898, No 473 was soon repainted into the umber livery of the LBSCR in the early 20th century and is seen here waiting to leave Horsted Keynes in the mid-1960s. *Bluebell Archive (Ken Chown)*

FOUNDATIONS OF THE MODERN BLUEBELL RAILWAY The late 1960s and 1970s saw several events that collectively set the Bluebell Railway on course for the future. The first of these was purchase of the track between Sheffield Park and Horsted Keynes from British Railways, achieved in 1968 after several years of intense fundraising during which the line was only rented and the railway lived somewhat from day to day. The second was the arrival at the railway of several locomotives and other rolling stock belonging to independent preservation groups, including the Bulleid Society and what is now the Maunsell Locomotive Society. Mostly larger than those already at the railway, these locomotives have proved crucial in running the longer trains that the railway now needs to operate.

The first larger locomotive at the Bluebell Railway was BR Standard Class 5 No 75027, which arrived in working order in January 1969 direct from BR service at the end of steam in North West England. It provided welcome relief for the smaller engines that had run the service through the 1960s. Soon after, in September 1971, the Bulleid Society brought its SR 'West Country' Class locomotive No 21C123 *Blackmoor Vale* to the railway and set about repairing it for service.

Left: SR Class 'S15' No 847 is navigated carefully through the local roads by a specialist haulage team in mid-October 1978.

Left: A few days earlier, SR Class 'Q' No 30541 made a similar journey, photographed near Cuckfield on 5 October 1978.

Right: Travelling in convoy with No 30541 was BR Class 9F No 92240, which had been purchased by a group of Locomotive Department members from Barry scrapyard. It is pictured here on arrival at Sheffield Park. *All Bluebell Archives (P. D. Nicholson)*

BLACKMOOR VALE RETURNS TO STEAM No 21C123 made Bluebell Railway history on 15 May 1976 when it entered service after several years of restoration. Bulleid Society and Carriage & Wagon Department members also restored two Bulleid carriages for the occasion. With others already in service, the railway was able to celebrate the occasion by recreating the Southern Railway's classic named train, the 'Atlantic Coast Express', which left Waterloo at 11.0am for seaside destinations in Devon and Cornwall. This was the railway's first big celebration of a locomotive's return to service. One of the 'ACE' services on that special weekend is pictured here ready to depart from Sheffield Park. *Roger Price*

Sheffield Park Station

Right: **SHEFFIELD PARK STATION**, seen here on 2 August 2018, is painted in the colours of the LBSCR, the company that ran the line from its opening. The stained glass in the porch was reinstated in 2017. *John Sandys*

Below: This was the view of the station looking north from the footbridge on 26 January 2019. The railway's talisman locomotive, SECR 'P' Class No 323 *Bluebell*, sits in Platform 1. As much as possible of the original station has been preserved, although, as the headquarters of the railway, there has been considerable development over the past 60 years to turn it from a wayside station into a busy railway terminus. Among these changes was the building of a restaurant and a shop on Platform 1, and a museum located on Platform 2 (see page 12). The canopies on both platforms have also been extended back to their original length and their zinc sheeting renewed after 130 years of service. Sheffield Park is home to the railway's locomotive works, shed and SteamWorks exhibition (see page 14). *John Sandys*

Below: The station takes on a new character after dark, softly lit by authentic gas lamps. On 4 January 2015, coaching stock stands silently in the platform but the signal cabin is still busy. *Jonathan Horrocks*

Left: **BOOKING HALL** Passengers find a friendly welcome in the booking hall, but getting a glimpse of the booking clerk behind the original ticket windows is tricky as they are small and low. *Derek Hayward*

Below left: **SHEFFIELD PARK NORTH** SR Class 'Q' No 30541 stands in Platform 1 on 24 August 2016 with a northbound service. The carriage behind the locomotive is SECR No 3360, which has been converted for disabled access (see p36). *Jonathan Horrocks*

Below: **SHEFFIELD PARK SIGNAL BOX** Unusually, the signal cabin at Sheffield Park is situated on the former down platform, which gives passengers the chance to watch the signalman at work while they wait for their train. The illuminated detector light in the station diagram above the instrument shelf shows that the Platform 1 track is currently occupied. *Keith Leppard*

Left: **EARLY START** The original enclosed timber footbridge at the north end of Sheffield Park station was demolished in the 1940s, leaving passengers to use a foot crossing. Forty years later, the Bluebell put up a replacement at the southern end of the station that had previously been located at Lingfield station, on the route north from East Grinstead towards London. The footbridge now provides an excellent vantage point from which to view train movements at the station. In this early morning view, LBSCR 'Terrier' No 55, temporarily in BR livery as No 32655, simmers in Platform 2 on 14 January 2012 with a single-coach train formed of SECR 'Birdcage' Brake No 3363. These carriages get their nickname from the raised glazed section in the roof over the guard's accommodation. An elevated seat allows the guard a view forward and back to monitor the security of the train while in motion. *Dave Bowles*

Right: **SHEFFIELD PARK SOUTH** From the footbridge, the south end of Sheffield Park station is laid out before you. Originally, track continued beyond the buffer stops in the far distance over the A275 and onwards to Newick and Lewes. On 24 March 2019, SR Class 'S15' No 847 is just south of Platform 2, passing SR Class 'U' No 31618. The latter locomotive has been out of service since 1994, awaiting major overhaul. The original water tower on the right supplies water columns on both the platforms. Meanwhile the new locomotive maintenance shed, built as part of the ASH project with support from the National Lottery Heritage Fund, is taking shape in the background; it was completed in Summer 2019. *John Sandys*

Left: **SHEFFIELD PARK** On 12 October 2018 trains are seen in both of the station platforms with locomotives at their northern ends. This is only possible if the last train to arrive has a second locomotive already attached at the rear or if a station pilot is available to release the train engine so it can move past the coaches and return to the north end of the train. SR Class 'S15' No 847 and Class 'Q' No 30541 stand in the weak afternoon sunshine that is lighting up the station buildings and nameboard. *Jonathan Horrocks*

Right: **NORTHBOUND DEPARTURE** Both platforms at Sheffield Park have viewing areas extending north from the platforms that let visitors get a good view of departing trains. On 21 May 2011 SECR Class 'P' No 178 and Class 'C' No 592 begin the journey to Horsted Keynes by crossing the Prime Meridian that runs past the end of the platforms. No 178 carries the ornate fully lined SECR passenger livery, complete with company crest on the tanks, while No 592 is in the only marginally less ornate good livery of that company. *Keith Leppard*

Railway Heritage

A visit to the Bluebell Railway is so much more than a train ride. Great attention is paid to creating an experience of a bygone era, from the detail of the staff uniforms to the dressing of the stations with period advertisements and accessories.

Below: **A TICKET TO TREASURE** Traditional Edmondson tickets, which the Bluebell produces using an original printing machine, were introduced in the 1840s and used on Britain's railways through to 1990. Tickets are pre-printed on stiff card rectangles, each with a unique serial number, and are date-stamped by the booking clerk at the time of sale. This picture shows the date-stamping process and (inset) a ticket for an adult 3rd Class return trip from Sheffield Park to Kingscote. *Keith Leppard*

Above: **RAILWAY MUSEUM** A new museum opened in 2012, housed in an extension to the former up platform waiting room at Sheffield Park. It was built as part of a project funded by the Heritage Lottery Fund to provide covered storage for the railway's operating carriages behind Platform 2. The museum's displays show smaller artefacts and interpret railway operations for visitors. *Keith Leppard*

Right: **RED FOR DANGER** A signal box, originally located at Withyam on the former east-west route from East Grinstead to Eridge, has been re-erected at the north end of the museum. It contains a small lever frame that visitors can try out under supervision while watching the trains depart. SR 'U' Class No 1638 is seen here leaving the station on 17 September 2012. *Keith Leppard*

MIXED TRAFFIC As well as preserving heritage locomotives and rolling stock, the railway also aims to conserve and demonstrate modes of railway operation from the past. Here SECR 'P' Class No 178 (built in 1910) hauls a mixed train typical of railway operations on branch lines in the Victorian and Edwardian eras; it includes LBSCR 1st No 661 (1880), LCDR Brake 3rd No 114 (1889) and assorted wagons. The train is approaching Horsted Keynes on 12 March 2011. *Keith Leppard*

Historic Locomotives

The Bluebell collection spans almost 90 years of development of the railway steam locomotive in the UK from the oldest – LBSCR 'Terrier' No 672 *Fenchurch*, an example of designs from the mid-Victorian era that was built in 1872 – through to a member of the last steam locomotive class to be built for Britain's railways, BR Class 9F No 92240, which left Crewe Works in 1958.

Left: **No 4 SHARPTHORN** This diminutive locomotive has never steamed on the Bluebell Railway yet holds a unique and crucial place in its history. Built in 1877, it was used by the original contractors during the construction of the line in 1882. A century later it was brought to the Bluebell and is pictured here at Horsted Keynes where it is normally on display. *Derek Hayward*

Below: **SHEFFIELD PARK YARD** This aerial view, taken on 29 March 2012, shows the yard backed by the running shed, locomotive works and, on the right 'Atlantic House'. 'E4' No B473 is in the foreground and 'P' Class tanks Nos 178 and 323 to the right. To the left are No 3 *Captain Baxter* behind diesel shunter No 13236, and Class 4 tank No 80151. At the back are the boilerless engine of 'S15' No 847, in works for major overhaul at the time, and the engine of 'Q' Class No 541 with the tender from 'U' Class No 1618. The large locomotive in the centre behind B473 is 9F No 92212, visiting from the Mid-Hants Railway at the time. *Martin Lawrence*

Below: **NORTH LONDON RAILWAY No 2650** Built at Bow Works in 1880, this locomotive arrived at the railway in working order in 1962. It also has a unique role in Bluebell history as it was loaned to contractors who were dismantling the line north from Horsted Keynes in 1964. After many years out of use, it was returned to service in its BR livery as No 58850 from 1984 to 1993, in time for it to play an important part in the Bluebell's rebuilding of that same route. It is pictured here at Horsted Keynes. *Bluebell Archive*

In 2018, the railway opened its SteamWorks interactive exhibition at Sheffield Park to present and explain its precious collection of locomotives to visitors, with funding from the National Lottery Heritage Fund. Not all of the locomotives in the collection can be kept operational at any given time as repairing one now costs several hundred thousand pounds and takes a lot of time. So, locomotives are overhauled to meet the operating needs of the railway while the rest are stored waiting their turn for repair. With the adjacent running shed housing further locomotives not in use at the time, visitors can now view many of the historic locomotives in the collection. They can also find out how a locomotive works.

Above: **LBSCR 'A1X' 'TERRIER' No 55 STEPNEY** with No 3 *Captain Baxter* behind, on display in SteamWorks in March 2019. *Keith Leppard*

Left: **BR CLASS 4 4-6-0 No 75027** sits behind No 3 *Captain Baxter* in the SteamWorks exhibition in March 2019. On the left is the *Stepney* simulator, where visitors can experience a driver's-eye view of a trip up the line. *Keith Leppard*

Above: **PRE-GROUPING GEMS** LSWR Radial Tank No 488 (built in 1885) sits at Sheffield Park in August 1973 with the LBSCR Directors' Saloon No 60. Considered to be among the gems of the railway's collection, sadly both have been out of use for many years. *Bluebell Archive (S. C. Nash)*

Below: **FENCHURCH** LBSCR 'Terrier' No 72, in the livery it carried at the railway for most of the years up until 2001, is pictured at Horsted Keynes with the GNR Directors' Saloon during the 1980s under the admiring gaze of a young visitor. *Bluebell Archive (David Christie)*

Above: **LBSCR VETERANS** More recently seen on the line in BR lined black and SR lined olive-green liveries, perennial favourite 'E4' 0-6-2T No 473 *Birch Grove* is pictured here at Sheffield Park in 2002 paired with 'A1' No 672 *Fenchurch*, both in the LBSCR's umber livery of the early 1900's. *Keith Leppard*

Below: **SLEEPING GIANTS** In 2005/06, 30 years after the structure was first erected, the locomotive running shed was completed with a brick side wall that includes windows to a traditional design. Here two out-of-service locomotives, BR Standard Class 4MT No 75027 and Class 9F No 92240, stand outside the shed in October 2010. *Keith Leppard*

Left: SR 'USA' CLASS No 30064 This locomotive is of a North American design and was bought by the Southern Railway at the end of the Second World War. It came to the Bluebell in 1971 and entered service immediately, working until 1984 with only a brief pause for overhaul. Seen here in a BR-style green livery, it is now displayed in War Department grey as No WD1959, awaiting its turn for repair. *Bluebell Archive*

Below left: SECR CLASS 'H' No 263 The powerful Class 'H' tank engines were built in the 1900s for heavy suburban traffic in south-east London and later migrated to country branch lines as electrification progressed. No 263 ended up very close to the Bluebell, working between East Grinstead and Three Bridges until 1964, when it was withdrawn. Coming to the Bluebell in 1975, it is pictured here on 28 July 2012, immaculately turned out in fully lined SECR passenger livery as it began its third period of service on the railway. *Martin Lawrence*

Below: SR 'V' CLASS 'SCHOOLS' No 928 STOWE The 'Schools' Class was designed originally to operate the route from London to Hastings via Tonbridge, which had an exceptionally narrow loading gauge because of short-cuts taken during its construction. Introduced in 1930, the 'Schools' were the most powerful 4-4-0 locomotives ever built and proved so successful that in the end they were used widely across the Southern network. No 928 *Stowe* arrived at the Bluebell in 1980 and operated for much of that decade, being seen here at Three Arch Bridge on the approach to Horsted Keynes. *Bluebell Archive (David Christie)*

Heavy engineering

Keeping steam locomotives running requires a host of heavy engineering skills and facilities that were commonplace in Britain during the steam era but nowadays are a niche market at best. The Bluebell – in common with other preserved lines – has to scour the country and beyond for commercial fabrication of parts as well as doing a multitude of engineering tasks in-house. The locomotive works at Sheffield Park was built in 1975 and, although extended twice, is still too small to cope with all the work required; much of this is still done outside in the yard.

Below: **BOILER REPAIRS** Locomotives require a heavy overhaul after every 10 years of service. The boiler is removed from the frames, inspected and repaired to satisfy the boiler inspector. At the same time, other necessary repairs will be done to the engine (cylinders, motion, frames, etc) to give hopefully 10 more years of reasonably trouble-free use. Here the boiler from SECR 'H' Class No 263 is under repair during 2011, with SR Class 'S15' No 847's boiler in the background. *Bluebell Archive (David Phillips)*

Above right: **RESTORATION PROJECT** BR Standard Class 4 tank No 80100 is one of only three steam locomotives at the railway never to have operated there. Pictured in the running shed in August 2010 during the railway's 50th anniversary celebrations, it is still in the condition in which it arrived in 1978 from a scrapyard in South Wales, where it had spent more than a decade. It makes quite a contrast with its sister locomotive No 80064 (posed behind it) and No 80151 seen in the next picture; restoring a locomotive from this condition to working order is a major task! *Derek Hayward*

Right: **NEARING COMPLETION** The third BR Standard Class 4 tank at the railway, No 80151, has seen considerable use. In April 2019 its latest overhaul was nearing completion as its completed boiler was craned back into the chassis. From this point, finishing the overhaul took only three months; it re-entered service in July 2019. *Roger Cruse*

Below: **BUILDING BR CLASS 2 TANK No 84030** Not quite a new build, but pretty close, is the conversion of former BR Class 2 tender locomotive No 78059 into its tank engine equivalent, 2-6-2T No 84030 none of which was preserved. On 26 July 2018 the heavily modified frames were lowered onto the driving wheels, a significant milestone in the project. The front of the frames is on the left, indicated by the smokebox saddle and the cylinders. *Tony Sullivan*

BUILDING FROM NEW The biggest locomotive engineering project undertaken on the Bluebell Railway to date is the construction of a new Class 'H2' LBSCR 'Atlantic' (the railway term for a 4-4-2 wheel arrangement). Pictured in 2018/19, a brand new set of frames, cylinders and motion is complete (*above, Jonathan Horrocks*) with cab (*above right, David Jones*) and now awaits its boiler, which has been modified and refurbished from a Great Northern Railway locomotive. By 14 August 2019, that was outside the erecting shed awaiting hydraulic and steam testing for its insurance certificate while the tank for its new tender was being delivered (*right, David Jones*). It's never wise to predict when such a major project will be finished, but the day when No 32424 *Beachy Head* is steamed is definitely getting close.

POLEAY BRIDGE Leaving Sheffield Park the railway crosses the River Ouse, then Poleay Bridge, where views of trains taken from the west, particularly in the late afternoon, are a favourite with the railway's many lineside photographers. Here SECR 'C' Class No 592, reflected in the flood from the river, departs with a train formed of BR Mark I and SR Bulleid stock on 17 January 2010. *Jon Bowers*

Left: **FRESHFIELD BANK** The journey to Horsted Keynes, which takes about 15 minutes, is uphill most of the way. Following the River Ouse upstream from Sheffield Park, crews quickly have to tackle Freshfield Bank, which, at a gradient of 1 in 75, is steep in railway terms.
SR 'U' Class No 1638 gets to grips with the ascent on a heavy 'Santa Special' working in December 2009. *Ian Wright*

Below left: **FRESHFIELD BANK** BR Class 5MT No 73082 *Camelot,* which was named in 1959 following the withdrawal of the 'King Arthur' Class locomotive of that name, is starting the climb in an undated picture taken between 1995 and 2000. During the 1990s the railway operated a set of BR Mark I coaches in maroon livery. This livery was used throughout much of the UK from the mid-1950s, with locomotives in lined black or Brunswick green, until British Railways switched to blue and grey livery at the end of steam in the late 1960s. *Bluebell Archive*

TREMAINS In April 2011, wending their way through woodlands near Tremains, midway between Sheffield Park and Horsted Keynes, lucky passengers on a southbound 'Bluebell Special' get to see just how the railway got its name. The train is hauled, appropriately, by SECR Class 'P' No 323 *Bluebell*. *Andrew Strongitharm*

Above: **TOWARDS KETCHES WOOD** Almost 20 years after the picture on the previous page, BR Class 5 No 73082 *Camelot* is again in charge of a northbound train. Camelot was built in 1955 and so is one of the youngest locomotives at the railway. It is pictured heading towards Ketches Wood and Freshfield Bank on 20 October 2015. The locomotive had just undergone a 10-year heavy overhaul and was on test prior to entering service. The four carriages are BR Mark 1 design, also as in the previous picture, but are now in the carmine and cream livery of the early BR period rather than the later maroon livery. *Derek Hayward*

Right: **ROCK CUTTING** lies between the top of Freshfield bank and Tremains. The railway's LNWR Observation Car, built in 1913, provides passengers on a southbound service headed by No 323 *Bluebell* with a panoramic view of the autumn colours on 20 October 2015. *Derek Hayward*

Above: **TOWN PLACE** The line levels out between Town Place bridge and Tremains. Former LSWR Adams Radial Tank No 488, built in 1885 and running here in BR livery as No 30583, is approaching Freshfield Lane in the gentle light of late autumn 1983. *Bluebell Archive (Peter Zabek)*

Above: **SUSSEX FLASHBACK** SR Class 'U' No 1618 crosses Keysford Lane Bridge with a northbound service while a vintage bus passes below. This springtime scene was captured in 1983. *Bluebell Archive*

Below: **KEYSFORD LANE BRIDGE** No 488 has just passed Keysford Lane with a northbound train in 1988. The short-lived Holywell Halt was located here for the 1962 season. No 488 owes its survival to the demands of working the Lyme Regis branch, for which it and two sister engines were kept in service until the 1960s. Its LSWR pea green livery is contemporary with the salmon and bitter chocolate used on coach No 1520 (see page 38). *Bluebell Archive (Peter Constable)*

Below: **CASEFORD BRIDGE** Another 1 in 75 climb takes the line north towards Caseford Bridge and Horsted Keynes. The railway's former GWR 'Dukedog' Class locomotive No 9017 *Earl of Berkeley*, pictured here in GWR livery, passes with a northbound train in February 2005. *Paul Pettitt*

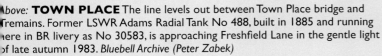

Left: **THREE ARCH BRIDGE** The distinctive form of Three Arch Bridge marks the start of the approach to Horsted Keynes. Northbound trains are still working hard as they pass the bridge, but here former LBSCR 'E4' No B473 is running with the grade on a southbound train formed mostly of SR Maunsell-era carriages. *Len Walton*

Below left: **THREE ARCH BRIDGE** On the approach to Horsted Keynes, the view of trains on the embankment between Three Arch Bridge and New Road Bridge in the afternoon light is another classic Bluebell scene. Here SECR Class 'O1' 0-6-0 No 65, rebuilt in 1908 from an 1896 SER Class 'O' design, heads north on 9 March 2009. At this time, No 65 was nearing the end of a 10-year period of very reliable service on the railway. Harry Wainwright's SECR designs shared several distinctive features and the 'O1' rebuild appears very similar to his own 'C' Class 0-6-0 design (see page 11), the most visible difference being the smaller tender of the 'O1', with external springs. *Jon Bowers*

Right: **APPROACHING HORSTED KEYNES** The weak sun of a winter afternoon catches the varnished teak of the railway's Metropolitan Railway coaches (see page 37) to great effect in this picture from 17 February 2008. GWR 'Dukedog' Class locomotive No 9017 *Earl of Berkeley* is leading its train across the embankment that forms the southern approach to Horsted Keynes station. *Derek Hayward*

Dinner is served

Below: **PULLMAN SERVICE** From the end of the 19th century, long-distance trains started to convey restaurant cars that offered meals served by waiters with all the style of the most reputable city eating establishments. This service reached its pinnacle in the opulent surroundings of the Pullman Cars, amply illustrated here by the interior of the Bluebell's 1st Class Parlour Kitchen Car *Fingall*, built in 1924, with tables laid for full service. *Richard Salmon*

Above and right: **PULLMAN STYLE** While 1st Class Pullman Cars were always known by name, their 3rd Class counterparts had numbers only. However, the 3rd Class Pullman in service at the Bluebell, formerly Car No 64 has been named *Christine*. Here guests are well into their lunch as the southbound 'Golden Arrow' passes Horsted Keynes on 12 August 2007. The interior of Christine shows that even Pullman 3rd class is quite sumptuous.
Both Keith Leppard

Below: **SERVICE WITH A SMILE**
Pullman service doesn't just include good food in extravagant surroundings. Welcome aboard! *Derek Hayward*

GOLDEN ARROW The Southern Railway's all-Pullman 'Golden Arrow' service, which operated from London to Dover for onward service to the continent, gained world-wide fame. This train is commemorated in the Bluebell Railway's own 'Golden Arrow' dining service.

Right: The up 'Arrow' passes the Kingscote distant signal in April 2008, hauled by 'West Country' Class 4-6-2 No 21C123 *Blackmoor Vale*. The distinctive air-smoothed casing of this type of locomotive, which was often used by the SR on the 'Golden Arrow', allows the train's insignia to be displayed to full effect.

Below: The up 'Arrow' is seen again in the second view, this time approaching Horsted Keynes on 25 July 2010 hauled by rebuilt 'Battle of Britain' Class 4-6-2 No 34059 *Sir Archibald Sinclair*.

Below right: Finally a down 'Golden Arrow' working approaches Horsted Keynes in the charge of BR Standard Class 4 tank No 80151 on 12 August 2007. *Paul Pettitt/Martin Lawrence/Keith Leppard*

Horsted Keynes station

HORSTED KEYNES is a large country station with five platforms, dock and goods yards. The railway's Carriage & Wagon Department is based there and a viewing gallery in the works is normally open to visitors.

Below: The station area viewed from the north in 2010. The line to Sheffield Park is in the centre, while the route of the former branch to Haywards Heath passes behind the signal box. When Bluebell services began, this branch was still being operated by British Railways electric trains. The Bluebell owns the trackbed of the branch as far as Ardingly and it is hoped that one day its operations will extend over this route too. *Keith Leppard*

Right: The station forecourt is seen here on 8 August 2015, with a classic GPO van on display for the day. The decorative tiling on the walls of the main station building is typical of traditional buildings in this part of Sussex. *Keith Leppard*

Below right: Pictured in the evening sunshine on 21 August 2005 southbound trains headed by BR Class 4 tank No 80151 and 'E4' Class No 32473 in BR livery stand at Platforms 3 and 4/5 respectively. The buildings and canopy on Platforms 1 and 2 were demolished by the LBSCR in 1914, and carefully reinstated between 1992 and 2005 to match the originals. *Jon Bowers*

Right: **PLATFORMS 3 AND 4** provide the focus for most of the passenger activity at Horsted Keynes. When trains on the single line cross there, the station becomes a temporary hive of activity. Between trains, passengers can linger at the bookstall or buffet, both of which are preservation items in their own right. On 23 May 2010 No 672 *Fenchurch* is providing brake van rides along the Ardingly spur. *Martin Lawrence*

Above right: **PERIOD DETAIL** Horsted Keynes station is preserved in the early Southern Railway period of c1930. Many artefacts help to recreate that bygone era. *Keith Leppard*

Right: Entering the booking hall on a winter's day is like stepping back in time, with an open coal fire to warm travellers. And in the adjacent waiting room there is a telephone where users had to press buttons A and B long before mobile phones were dreamed of! *John Sandys*

Left: **PERIOD SIGNAL BOX** Movements at Horsted Keynes are controlled from its magnificent signal box. Every one of its 40 levers is needed to control the station's complex track layout. On 17 May 2015 the fireman on SR Class 'Q' No 30541 prepares to hand over the single-line token as the northbound 'Golden Arrow' enters the station. *Keith Leppard*

Above and above right: **ELEPHANT PLAY VAN**
BR Scenery Van No 4601 was built in 1949 and later strengthened to convey elephants around the country with the rest of the Billy Smart's circus entourage. In 2015 an Arts Council Museum Resilience Fund grant was received to convert the van to provide a railway- (and elephant-) themed children's education and play facility. Opened in 2017 and pictured on 23 September 2019, the van sits in the dock at Horsted Keynes and is open when trains are running. *Both Martin Lawrence*

Right: **BRANCH-LINE DEPARTURE** When the picnic field at Horsted Keynes is open, accessed from Platform 1, it is the ideal spot to watch trains as they depart for Kingscote and East Grinstead. Here, SECR Class 'P' No 323 *Bluebell* and Class 'H' No 263 are in charge of a long train of vintage stock at the Branchline Weekend event, 19 May 2018. *Keith Leppard*

Left: **ONE FOGGY MORNING** On 21 September 2013 BR Standard Class 4 tank No 80151, one of the few Bluebell locomotives to face south, emerges from the fog as it approaches Horsted Keynes from the north. The locomotive is framed by two elegant bracket signals, which serve as the up starter signals for three of the four platforms, as it passes a rake of restored goods vans and open wagons in the up sidings. The platform water cranes are no longer in use, water for locomotives being provided instead by a small tank in the down yard. *Jon Bowers*

Right: **NORTHBOUND FROM HORSTED KEYNES** Viewed from a location on the east side of the railway not normally accessible to photographers, SR Class 'S15' No 847 makes a spirited departure from Horsted Keynes on 10 March 2015 with a photographers' charter. The low posts in the foreground carry the signal wires that operate the mechanical signals. These wires are connected via pulleys to levers in the signal box. In the era depicted at Horsted Keynes, all signals would have been operated in this way, including those at a considerable distance from the signal box. However, working these required a lot of strength to pull the lever and move the signal arm, so now the signals that are further from the box are moved by electric motors, though still controlled by signal levers in the traditional way. *Dave Bowles*

East Grinstead

2013

Mainline Rail

Hill Place Farm

Hill Place (Imberhorne) Viaduct

Imberhorne Lane Bridge

Hazelden Farm Bridge

Turners Hill Road Bridge

Vowels Lane Bridge

Kingscote

1994

Mill Place Bridge

Birch Farm Crossing

Birchstone Bridge

Ingwersen's

New Coombe Bridge

Site of West Hoathly station

1992

West Hoathly

Tunnel

Sharpthorne

Black Hut

Vaux Bri

Dates along the route indicate the first opening of the Bluebell to that point from the South (Sheffield Park)

Leamland Bridge

House
dge

1961

Horsted Keynes

New Road
Bridge

Three Arch
Bridge
('Nobles')

1960

Caseford
Bridge

Keysford Lane
Bridge ('Holywell
Waterworks')

Tremaines

Lindfield
Wood

Monteswood
Lane Bridge

Freshfield
Lane Bridge

Town Place
Bridge

Oakham
Bridge

Freshfieldbank

Ketches
Wood

Freshfield bank

River Ouse
flood plain

Poleay
Bridge

Ouse
Bridge

A2

Sheffield
Park 1960

Images from D Bowles, J Harwood, D Hayward, M Lawrence, K Leppard, P Pettitt, I Wright

Celebrations

There have been many special events at the Bluebell Railway over its first 60 years, arranged to mark special anniversaries, the bringing together of groups of locomotives or major achievements. Some of these events are featured in these pages.

Right: **GIANTS OF STEAM 2007** was the ideal chance to create a line-up of O. V. S. Bulleid's 'West Country'/'Battle of Britain' Class 4-6-2 locomotives. The Bluebell's own No 21C123 *Blackmoor Vale* and No 34028 *Eddystone*, at the railway for the year, stand with visiting locomotives Nos 34007 *Wadebridge* and 34081 *92 Squadron* at the north end of Horsted Keynes station against the setting sun on 19 October. *Derek Hayward*

Right: **'TERRIER' GALA 2006** Built in the 1870s, the LBSCR 'Terriers' are great survivors. As well as the Bluebell's Nos 55 *Stepney* and 672 *Fenchurch,* eight others still exist and in November 2006 three visitors joined the residents in a 'Terrier' gala. From the left, Nos 32678 (formerly *Knowle*), W8 *Freshwater* (formerly No 646 *Newington*) and 662 *Martello* pose with *Stepney* and *Fenchurch* at the north end of Horsted Keynes station. *Jon Bowers*

Right: **50th ANNIVERSARY OF THE BLUEBELL, 6-8 AUGUST 2010** A recreation of the railway's first public train departs from Sheffield Park. No 55 *Stepney* is in its 1960 livery, while coaches Nos 1098 and 6686 substitute for the original Nos 320 and 6575. At the rear of the train No 672 *Fenchurch* stands in for No 323 *Bluebell*, which was not in service at the time. *Derek Hayward*

Right: The traditional celebratory cavalcade of all available locomotives at Horsted Keynes. From left to right they are LBSCR Nos 55 *Stepney* and 672 *Fenchurch*, SECR Nos 178 and 592, 'E4' No B473, Class 'U' No 1638 and No 34059 *Sir Archibald Sinclair*. When this many locomotives all whistle together they can really make themselves heard! *Martin Lawrence*

Carriage craftsmanship

The Bluebell's collection contains some 80 carriages that span a century of design development. Only the earliest arrivals, together with some of the newer BR Mark 1 coaches that came later, were in a condition fit to run and these all required major work within a decade or so. Others were derelict, often lacking their interior fittings and, for most of the Victorian coaches, their underframes and running gear too. So far, only two-thirds of them have been used in passenger service, mostly following extensive rebuilding and restoration.

Below: **CARRIAGE WORKS** Carriages comprise a body frame clad with external and internal panelling, mounted on an underframe. The wheels are either directly mounted on the underframe – the earliest design – or carried on two bogies that swivel at either end of the coach. This view of the Horsted Keynes carriage works, taken from the public viewing area in 2011, shows work completed on the framework of LBSCR four-wheel Brake 3rd No 949, originally constructed in 1881. *Keith Leppard*

Above: **SECR No 3360** Railway coachbuilding continued the tradition of craftsmanship found in the horse-drawn carriages that were being superseded, and these traditions are maintained by the Bluebell's Carriage & Wagon Department today. During 2010/11 No 3360 was converted to provide a saloon for disabled visitors, with support from The Big Lottery Fund through its 'People's Millions' programme. It carries SECR crimson lake livery, contemporary with the ornate lined green seen on the railway's SECR locomotives. A coach will need at least 15 coats of paint, filler and varnish to produce a finish you can see your reflection in. *Keith Leppard*

Right: **CARRIAGE WORKS** The oldest railway coaches were made entirely of timber, but by the end of the 19th century underframes were being made of steel, and steel panelling started to be used soon after; body framing switched to steel from the 1950s onwards. No matter how well a steel-panelled coach is cared for, eventually its panelling will need replacement. Here, work progresses on re-panelling SR Bulleid Brake 3rd No 2526. Built in 1951, the coach entered traffic on the Bluebell in 2009. *Richard Salmon*

METROPOLITAN RAILWAY COACHES In 1961 the railway acquired a set of four coaches built in 1898/1900 that had most recently been operating on the Chesham branch of the London Underground's Metropolitan Line. Their arrival added much-needed passenger capacity and they bore the brunt of the traffic until around 1968, when their increasing dilapidation caused them to be laid aside. After many years of work the two outer coaches of the set, Brake 3rd No 387 and Full 3rd No 394, were returned to traffic in 1999; Composite 1st/3rd No 368 followed in 2002, and Composite No 412 completed the set in 2006.

These coaches returned to the Metropolitan Line in central London in January 2013 as part of steam-hauled special trains to celebrate the 150th anniversary of the London Underground and have since been back for further special events.

Top right: No 412 is seen at Kingscote on 12 August 2007 displaying an exquisite varnished teak finish. *Keith Leppard*

Right: The interiors of all but the newest (55-year-old!) coaches tend to be visions of richly varnished woodwork, brightly polished brass or chrome fittings and padded seating trimmed in moquette to an authentic pattern.

Here we see 1st Class and 3rd Class compartments of No 412. In addition to a carpet, 1st Class passengers get wider and more deeply padded seats, sitting four-a-side rather than five. The wood trim and ceiling finishes are also richer. *Keith Leppard/Martin Lawrence*

Above: **SOUTHERN RAILWAY No 1309** One of the earliest full carriage restorations at the Bluebell was that of SR Maunsell Open 3rd No 1309, built in 1935. Work was completed in 1984 and earned its restorers the prestigious Association of Railway Preservation Societies' Coach of the Year Award. It has since run almost continuously in public service. *Keith Leppard*

Right: **SOUTHERN RAILWAY No 1336**, built in 1933 by Richard Maunsell, provides 3rd Class accommodation in open saloons. With seats trimmed in Jazz pattern moquette, it was returned to traffic in 2008 following more than a decade of work. *Keith Leppard*

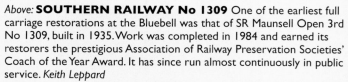

Above: **LONDON & SOUTH WESTERN RAILWAY No 1520,** a Brake 3rd, was built in 1910 and intended originally to carry passengers and their volumes of luggage on long-distance services. It entered traffic on the Bluebell in 2010 in the distinctive salmon and bitter chocolate livery of the LSWR after a 20-year restoration. Pictured at Kingscote, No 1520 displays a destination board appropriate to its origins; Bude was one of the seaside destinations at the far west of the LSWR route map. *Keith Leppard*

Right: The interior of No 1520 is as striking as the exterior, seen here on its first day in service on 7 August 2010. *Keith Leppard*

Above: **LBSCR BOGIE 1ST No 7598** Built in 1903, this is the only example at the railway of an LBSCR bogie coach for normal passenger use. Restoration took a decade, including provision of a replacement underframe; it entered service in 1999. Requiring some further work in the late 2000s, it is pictured here in fully lined early SR livery soon after its return to traffic in May 2012. *Keith Leppard*

Right and below right: **LBSCR FOUR-WHEEL 1ST No 661** This was the first four-wheel coach to be restored to use at the railway. Built by Stroudley in 1880, No 661 is from the same era as the railway's 'Terrier' locomotives, *Stepney* and *Fenchurch*. Its coach body had survived since 1924, minus underframe and wheels, incorporated into a house. Representing the previous generation of 1st Class provision to that offered by No 7598, No 661 entered service at the railway in 2004. It is pictured here in two views from 2007. *Both Keith Leppard*

Left: **SR SEMI-OPEN BRAKE 3RD No 2526** The Bluebell operates several examples of coaches to designs by O. V. S. Bulleid for the Southern Railway in the 1940s. Considerably more modern than coaches of the previous Maunsell era, their production continued after the 1948 nationalisation and many of their design features were continued in the later BR Standard Mark 1 coaches that also feature in the Bluebell's working fleet. No 2526 entered Bluebell service in 2009 following a lengthy restoration and is pictured at Horsted Keynes in February 2010. The wisp of steam is from a leak in the steam heating system. *Keith Leppard*

Right: **A ROUTE REDISCOVERED** A quarter of a century on from the dismantling of the original line north from Horsted Keynes, the trackbed was so overgrown as to be barely visible in many places, and had structures built on it for farm use in others. Nature had clearly reasserted itself in this view taken at Horsted House Farm on 6 May 1989. *Mike Esau*

Left: **NORTH OF LEAMLAND BRIDGE** Thoughts of extending the railway back to East Grinstead began in 1974, when the chance arose to purchase the former West Hoathly station site, but work on the ground only began in 1988 once legal issues had been sorted out and the railway had managed to secure the part of the trackbed immediately north of Horsted Keynes. Here, the railway's Ransoms & Rapier steam crane is in use for the ceremonial start of tracklaying north of Leamland Bridge on 13 March 1988. *Mike Esau*

Right: **HORSTED HOUSE FARM SHUTTLE** Public services over the first mile of the extension to Horsted House Farm bridge began in the spring of 1990. Trains were formed of two Maunsell carriages, the northern one – a Brake Composite – being adapted to allow 'push-pull' working. SECR 'P' Class locomotive No 323 *Bluebell* is pictured at the then northern limit of the line with the first train on the first full day of operations, 19 May 1990. *Mike Esau*

Left: **THROUGH SHARPTHORNE TUNNEL** To reach West Hoathly, the next target of the extension, the route to and through Sharpthorne Tunnel, had to be reinstated. This work was completed in time for No 35027 *Port Line* to break the banner at the official opening of the tunnel on 16 May 1992. With public attention at the time focused on the construction of the Channel Tunnel, it seemed only right that the Bluebell's own version of the 'Golden Arrow' service, which famously linked London and Paris, should have the honour. *Mike Esau*

Below left: **WEST HOATHLY** A temporary run-round loop was provided at West Hoathly so that the regular trains from Sheffield Park could run through to this new terminus, although since no station was established – a condition of the planning consent for the extension – passengers could not alight from the train. SR Class 'S15' No 847 is pictured at this temporary terminus on 22 May 1993. *Bluebell Archive (R. Bamberough)*

Right: **NEW COOMBE BRIDGE** A significant gap in the route just north of West Hoathly, where a brick-arch underbridge had been demolished after British Railways closed the line, had to be filled for the extension to reach Kingscote. Here one of three spans of a steel girder bridge is craned into position on 10 May 1993 as the push north continues. Trains began running over the last part of the 4 miles from Horsted Keynes to Kingscote on 23 April 1994. *Mike Esau*

Horsted Keynes to Kingscote

Left: **VAUX END** From Horsted House Farm the line continues climbing to Vaux End, where the Maunsell Locomotive Society's SR 'Q' Class was pictured on 18 April 2019. Built in 1939, the locomotive returned to service after overhaul in 2015, running in BR livery as No 30541. Here it is heading a northbound train formed of the railway's vintage Metropolitan Railway carriages with, immediately behind the locomotive, London Chatham & Dover Railway four-wheel Brake 3rd No 114 of 1889, which entered traffic following restoration in 2006. *Dave Bowles*

Above right: **LEAMLAND BRIDGE** crosses the line at the northern end of the Horsted Keynes station area. With both main and loop lines extending some distance beyond the bridge, the section has the appearance of double track. In this picture, SECR Class 'P' No 178 and Class 'C' No 592 double-head a northbound train formed of SR stock of the Bulleid and Maunsell eras on 21 May 2011. No 178 is the third of the railway's 'P' Class tanks. Unlike Nos 27 and 323 *Bluebell*, it had to wait many years before finally being restored and entering service at the railway for the first time in 2010. *Keith Leppard*

Right: **HORSTED HOUSE FARM CROSSING** The line continues to climb steeply from Horsted Keynes, leaving behind the river valleys to reach the Wealden plateau. Class 'E4' No 3473 makes a fine sight as it heads a northbound train towards Horsted House Farm crossing on 20 February 2010. Next to the locomotive is a six-wheel milk tanker, built in 1933 for express dairy traffic from the West Country to London. Behind it is SECR 3rd Class coach No 1098; built in 1922 for suburban traffic, its 10 compartments are each intended to accommodate 10 passengers (hence the nickname '100 seater'), although this is a tight squeeze – the commuter's lot perhaps hasn't changed so much! *Keith Leppard*

Right: **HORSTED HOUSE FARM BRIDGE** From the footpath crossing, the line enters a cutting that leads to Horsted House Farm occupation bridge, where SECR Class 'C' No 592 is pictured on a very snowy 19 December 2009. *Jon Bowers*

Below: **BLACK HUT** North of Horsted House Farm bridge, the route follows a series of twists and cuttings, passing Vaux End and Black Hut to reach Sharpthorne Tunnel. For many years out of bounds to lineside photographers, this section is not pictured so often as other parts of the route. BR Standard Class 4 No 75027 pilots No 34028 *Eddystone* on a northbound charter in 2006. *Jon Bowers*

Below right: **SHARPTHORN TUNNEL** The railway's 'E4' tank, in BR livery as No 32473, is pictured here on 28 April 2008 leaving the southern portal of the tunnel on another photographers' charter. The leading coaches are in the carmine and cream livery of the early days of British Railways. Commonly known as 'blood and custard', this livery didn't wear well and was later replaced by green on the Southern Region and maroon elsewhere. *Jon Bowers*

Left: **WEST HOATHLY** At the north end of Sharpthorne Tunnel the line levels out and passes through the site of the former West Hoathly station. This represents a fine vantage point to watch the trains pass. With the sun high in the west to light up the cutting, GWR 'Dukedog' No 9017 *Earl of Berkeley* heads north with the Metropolitan set on 10 October 2009. Built in 1938 from parts obtained from much older 'Duke' and 'Bulldog' classes, this locomotive came to the Bluebell in 1962 and has since had several periods of service on the line. *Derek Hayward*

Below left: Some of the platform-face brickwork is still visible, but most traces of West Hoathly station had gone by the time the railway acquired the site. SR Class 'U' No 1638 storms through with a rake of BR Mark 1 coaches in February 2015. *Keith Leppard*

Below: **BIRCH FARM CROSSING** From West Hoathly to Kingscote, the northbound gradient is gently falling and the line passes through woodlands with glimpses of the rolling fields beyond. Rebuilt 'Battle of Britain' Class No 34059 *Sir Archibald Sinclair* rounds the curve towards Birch Farm foot crossing with a heavy northbound train on a fine spring day, 26 April 2009. *Derek Hayward*

Left: **BIRCH FARM CROSSING** From Birch Farm there is a short uphill run into Kingscote. No B473 (LBSCR 'E4' Class No 473 in its early Southern Railway livery) is seen here with a matching set of SR carriages heading south past the crossing on 24 October 2010. *Keith Leppard*

Below left: **BIRCHSTONE BRIDGE**, the final overbridge before reaching Kingscote, makes a fine backdrop to views of southbound trains. LBSCR 'A1' No 672 *Fenchurch* is seen here with an Observation Car special in October 2010. Built in 1872, *Fenchurch* is the railway's oldest locomotive. It came to the railway in 1964 and ran in several guises before being rebuilt to its original 'A1' appearance in 2001 for further service. *Dave Bowles*

Below: **FORMER KINGSCOTE SIGNAL CABIN** The single-line points are located some distance south of Kingscote station; until February 2016, a signalman was based there in a small cabin. Rebuilt 'Battle of Britain' Class No 34059 *Sir Archibald Sinclair* passes the cabin with a train of BR Mark 1 carriages on 30 April 2011. Built in 1947, this locomotive was originally very similar to No 21C123 *Blackmoor Vale* but was rebuilt to a more conventional appearance (and mechanical design) in 1960. *Martin Lawrence*

BLUEBELL IN SPRING On a beautiful spring day in May 2012, Southern Railway Class 'U' No 1638 makes a fine sight as it takes its northbound six-coach train, in 1930s SR lined olive green livery, past a bank of spring flowers near Birchstone Bridge, between Horsted Keynes and Kingscote. *Paul Pettitt*

Keeping things moving

As well as the historic locomotives, carriages and stations, a visit to the Bluebell is about the people who make it all happen. The staff, from those in the public eye such as locomotive crew, guards, station staff, signalmen, and in the shops and buffet to those toiling behind the scenes on track, locomotive, carriage and signal maintenance, are mostly volunteers.

Above: **FOOTPLATE DUTIES** During 2007 rebuilt SR 'West Country' Class Bulleid 'Pacific' No 34028 *Eddystone* was operating at the railway on extended loan. These images show a view of the footplate on 15 July and the crew at Horsted Keynes on 12 August, with single-line token in hand. *Jon Bowers/Keith Leppard*

Below: **HEAVY WORK** Building and maintaining the infrastructure of the line can be heavy work, and often has to take place in locations remote from the road. The railway owns a 45-ton Ransomes & Rapier steam breakdown crane, built in 1942, which was based during its working life at Gorton and Newton Heath depots in Manchester. It has been used on a variety of tasks since arriving at the Bluebell in 1981 and is seen here removing a large redundant signal post from the lineside on Freshfield Bank in April 1987. *Tony Sullivan*

ght and far right top:
**RAFFIC AND
IGNALS** In July 2007
e guard on a southbound
ervice at Horsted Keynes
ves the 'right away' to
e loco crew, while in
eptember 2012 (*bottom
ft*) the platform staff at
heffield Park indicate
at a northbound train is
eady to depart. Access for
ains onto each single-line
ection is controlled by
 token, and in the third
cture (*Below left*) the
rew of a northbound
ervice exchange the
outhern section token for
e northern one with the
lorsted Keynes signalman
n 22 January 2012.
*n Bowers/Keith Leppard/
lartin Lawrence*

ight and far right bottom:
**MAINTAINING
THE TRACK** This is a
ever-ending task, carried
ut in all weathers. On a
nowy 6 April 2008 three
ardy souls do some
outine maintenance at
ngwersen's curve, while
mid the distractions of
 beautiful spring day on
8 May 2006 the track on
reshfield bank receives
ttention. *Both Jon Bowers*

Wagons and Freight

EARLY MORNING GOODS The Bluebell collection includes many wagons of historic interest as well as some kept primarily to serve the railway's civil engineering needs. Although it carries no freight traffic today, the railway operates demonstration goods trains for the benefit of visitors and photographers, recreating what was once such an important aspect of railway operations. Pictured here on 13 September 2008, SECR centenarians Class 'O1' No 65 and Class 'C' No 592 ascend Freshfield Bank in the early-morning mist. *Dave Bowles*

elow: **HEAVY FREIGHT** The British Railways Class 9F was the ultimate development
* UK steam locomotive design for freight haulage, intended for working heavy mineral
affic. Here, the Bluebell's example, No 92240, which was restored from a scrapyard
reck during the 1980s, heads a train of engineering wagons near Ketches Wood in
*ctober 2002. *Jon Bowers*

Above: **GOODS IN SPRING** Class 'B4' 0-4-0T No 96 *Normandy* was
built by Adams in 1893 for moving freight around the LSWR network
at the docks in Southampton. It has far more power than you would
expect from its size, but it is not able to travel easily at line speed, even
though this is only 25mph, so is not often used on passenger trains.
Normandy is seen here heading south past Three Arch Bridge in 2006
on a goods working formed of pre-grouping wagons. *Paul Pettitt*

Above left: **No 3 *CAPTAIN BAXTER*** This industrial 0-4-0T, built in 1877, worked at a lime works adjacent to Betchworth station in Surrey until it came to the Bluebell in 1960. With its distinctive red livery, *Captain Baxter* is a favourite with younger visitors. Until it was fitted with a vacuum brake in 2012, it was only used for shunting and for hauling demonstration goods trains. It is pictured here just south of Kingscote in August 2010. *Derek Hayward*

Above right: **SECR CLASS 'O1' No 65** storms north from Caseford bridge towards Horsted Keynes with a mixed goods working on 20 February 2018. 0-6-0 tender engines were the classic British goods locomotive design. No 65 was a 1908 SECR rebuild by Wainwright of an 1896 SER Class 'O' locomotive and had a long life, only being withdrawn in 1961. *Dave Bowles*

Left: **BULLEID 'LIGHT PACIFIC'** No 21C123 *Blackmoor Vale* is seen here rounding the curve by Town Place Farm on a freight working during the 'Giants of Steam' event in October 2007. Oliver Bulleid designed these locomotives to have an unusually low axle loading (weight) for their power, intending them to be usable on most of the Southern Railway's routes, not just the main lines. They could therefore be found handling all manner of traffic. Their air-smoothed casing earned them the nickname 'Spamcans' after a brand of tinned meat that was popular at the time. Unfortunately, some of their innovative mechanical features proved less than reliable and about half were eventually rebuilt to the form represented at the Bluebell by No 34059 *Sir Archibald Sinclair*. Although the rebuilds were excellent locomotives, their increased weight reduced their line availability, and they were not allowed west of Exeter. *Derek Hayward*

Right: **PICK-UP GOODS** In the days when every station had a goods yard and the railways were the universal carrier, required by law to carry any goods and parcels on demand, pick-up goods workings featured on any and every branch line. Wending their way from station to station, stopping each time to shunt the yard and pick up or deposit wagons there, these trains certainly took their time to get from A to B. In fine early spring sunshine, SECR 'P' Class No 178 recreates such a working, approaching Tremains with a northbound mixed goods train on 8 March 2011. *Martin Lawrence*

Left: **ENGINEERS' TRAIN** The low winter sun in February 2010 throws sharp shadows as No 9017 *Earl of Berkeley* takes a lengthy train of engineering wagons, normally used for carrying fresh or spent ballast, north past the abutments of the former Town House Farm occupation bridge, between Freshfield and Monteswood Lane bridges. When the railways were constructed, many bridges had to be provided to connect farm lands that had been bisected by the line. Over the years, as the ownership of the land changed, some of these, such as Town House, lost their original purpose, so when the bridge needed expensive repairs in the 1980s the decision was taken to demolish it and devote the money to other capital projects. *Jon Bowers*

Kingscote station

Right: **A PLATFORM RECREATED** When the railway took over the station site in 1985 it had been in use as a private house. The up platform and main station buildings were largely intact, but the down platform and its buildings had been demolished and the subway filled with rubble. Progressively these were reinstated. This picture shows the station in October 2014. *Keith Leppard*

Below: **KINGSCOTE** is about 4 miles north of Horsted Keynes. It is a delightful wayside station with two platforms and a small goods yard, lovingly preserved in the style of the 1950s British Railways period. The atmosphere on Platform 1 is captured in this view taken on 6 September 2019 as SR Class 'Q' No 30541 rolls into the station with a northbound service. There is no public parking allowed at Kingscote under the terms of the planning consent for the extended railway, so intending passengers must arrive by foot or cycle, or else reach the station using the trains. *John Sandys*

Right: **WARM WELCOME** At Kingscote, just as at Sheffield Park and Horsted Keynes, a traditional coal fire in the booking hall awaits travellers during a cold November day in 2012. *Martin Lawrence*

Left: **COUPLING UP** Between 1994 and 2013, when Kingscote served as the northern terminus of the line, large numbers of passengers periodically disrupted its tranquillity, watching while the locomotives ran around their trains. Here the crew of 'P' Class No 178 couple up for the journey south in front of an admiring audience. With trains now running on to East Grinstead, Kingscote is a through station again, which passengers visit to enjoy the goods yard display and picnic area, or just to soak up its sleepy charm. *Keith Leppard*

Below left: **STEAM WATCHING** Standing on Kingscote's down platform is one of the best places on the railway to take pictures of the trains from the east side. The railway's first locomotive, LBSCR 'A1X' No 55 *Stepney*, a perennial favourite with younger visitors thanks to its inclusion in Rev W. H. Awdry's stories, arrives with the first two of the Metropolitan Railway carriages to be restored, c1999. *Bluebell Archive (James Young)*

Below: While the driver takes a break, the railway's former LBSCR Class 'E4' tank No B473 sits in the crisp early sunshine on 24 October 2010 alongside a set of SR Maunsell coaches in matching livery. *Keith Leppard*

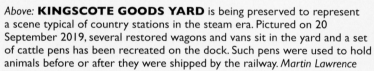

Above: **KINGSCOTE GOODS YARD** is being preserved to represent a scene typical of country stations in the steam era. Pictured on 20 September 2019, several restored wagons and vans sit in the yard and a set of cattle pens has been recreated on the dock. Such pens were used to hold animals before or after they were shipped by the railway. *Martin Lawrence*

Above right: **KINGSCOTE SIGNAL BOX** The original having been long-since demolished, the signal box was recreated in 1996 using one recovered from Brighton, placed on a newly built brick plinth. It was only fitted out and commissioned in February 2016. BR Standard tank No 80151 passes the box with a southbound service on 1 August 2018. *John Sandys*

Right: The box is fitted with an 'L' frame that has miniature levers. These operate signals and points electrically, rather than mechanically as happens at the other stations on the line. The 'L' frame was a later development in signal control and is appropriate to the era depicted at Kingscote. The signalman takes a break between trains on 15 August 2019. *John Sandys*

Extending North: 1994-2013

ght: **CLAY HEADS SOUTH** Having reached Kingscote in 1994, it took
other 20 years to complete the final 1.5 miles of the line to East Grinstead. By
the largest obstacle to overcome was the 100,000-ton mountain of domestic
bbish that had been dumped into a deep cutting at Imberhorne during the 1960s.
ith modern regulations to comply with, its removal represented not just a large
ysical barrier but also a huge cost. During 2004 tracks were laid from Kingscote
to the southern face of the tip and a considerable amount of inert clay was
moved for use elsewhere on the railway. Here, visiting Ivatt Class 2 tank
o 41312 is seen departing from the site with the first of these spoil trains on
May 2005. *Nigel Longdon*

low: **THE TRACK STOPPED HERE** A view of the southern tip face under
berhorne Lane bridge, taken in January 2009, shows the scale of the waste
ountain then blocking further progress northwards. The infill continued at the
ll height of a deepening cutting for 400 metres from here to the Hill Place Farm
erbridge. *Nigel Longdon*

Below: **NEW TRACKWORK** Although the first removal of waste from
the tip was by road, it proved more efficient to send the material out by rail.
To this end, trackwork was completed at the future East Grinstead station
and extended southwards over the viaduct to link the northern end of the tip
with the national rail network, re-establishing a connection that the railway
last enjoyed in 1964. This picture shows the newly installed track at the south
end of the station; the Network Rail connection is on the right. A Class 73
locomotive waits on Imberhorne Viaduct with the first train of empty wagons
for the waste removal operation on 3 July 2010. *Nigel Longdon*

Right: **RUBBISH HEADS NORTH** 1,000-ton train loads of waste from the cutting at Imberhorne departed daily for many weeks during 2011, each one costing about £25,000 to dispatch. This picture, taken in October 2011 from the Hill Place Farm occupation bridge at the northern end of the tip, shows waste being loaded into wagons for one of these trains; it also illustrates very well the industrial scale of the operation. *Gordon Callander*

Left: **INTO THE HOME STRAIGHT** Sufficient of the tip had been cleared by early 2012 to allow a single line cutting to be formed. During the rest of a very wet year, the remaining material was moved around, reprofiled and covered with some of the mountain of clay capping that had been stored on site. To accommodate more of this material, the cutting floor was raised and both approaches to it regraded. This view north from Imberhorne Lane bridge taken on 17 January 2013 shows the drainage being laid out in the virtually completed cutting. Just a couple of years earlier, a short walk on level ground could take someone from one side of this picture to the other. *John Sandys*

Right: **JOB DONE** After a monumental effort through a long cold winter, the railheads approaching the cutting from north and south were finally joined in a ceremony under Imberhorne Lane bridge on 8 March 2013. A week later, many of those most closely involved in the achievement posed for this commemorative picture, including the photographer (far right). *Mike Hopps*

Below: **PREPARING FOR REOPENING** After ballasting and levelling the completed track, the first steam locomotive since the closure and dismantling of the line some 50 years earlier finally arrived at East Grinstead from the south on 16 March 2013. Test trains were run over the subsequent days using various locomotives. On 21 March SECR Class 'H' No 263 is seen coming off the viaduct and into East Grinstead station on one of these workings. *Martin Lawrence*

Right: **FIRST SERVICE FROM EAST GRINSTEAD** The grand reopening of the railway from East Grinstead took place on 23 March 2013. The day dawned with very inclement weather, but went perfectly with large numbers of people enjoying the many special trains. Class 'E4' No B473 is pictured here passing south under Hill Place Farm bridge with the inaugural down train. This image represents the culmination of the Bluebell Railway's 40-year northern extension journey and is a testament to the work of so many who made it happen. The author was very lucky to be enjoying a seat in the front coach of this all-reserved train. *Mike Hopps*

Below right: The railway's first locomotive, No 55 *Stepney*, with No 323 *Bluebell* and No B473, had the honour of leading the empty stock working for the inaugural train into East Grinstead on 23 March 2013. This was the only occasion to date that *Stepney* has visited East Grinstead in Bluebell service; it was withdrawn from service in 2014. *Keith Leppard*

Kingscote to East Grinstead

Right: **NORTH OF KINGSCOTE** the route climbs steadily to the summit at Imberhorne cutting, passing through a narrow section of the formation where photography is not permitted. Just beyond this point, visiting SR Class 'V' No 925 *Cheltenham* pilots resident SR Class 'S15' No 847 on a northbound service amid the autumn colours during a 'Giants of Steam' weekend, 31 October 2015. Cheltenham contrasts with No 847 and the carriages, being painted in the malachite green livery developed by Oliver Bulleid after he took over from Richard Maunsell as the SR's Chief Mechanical Engineer in 1937. The rest of the train is in Maunsell's lined olive green livery. *Martin Lawrence*

Left: **IMBERHORNE CUTTING** Six years on from the reopening to East Grinstead, nature has largely regained control of the sides of the cutting that had been previously filled with rubbish. This view, taken on 31 August 2019, shows Southern Railway Class 'S15' No 847 passing through the cutting with a northbound train formed of SR Bulleid- and Maunsell-designed carriages. The location shown is very close to that of the trainload of rubbish seen on page 58 *John Sandys*

MBERHORNE VIADUCT The largest structure on the route between Kingscote and East Grinstead is Imberhorne Viaduct. The railway acquired it from British
ailways early in the extension process and it was refurbished well before the relaying of track. Its size and location make it very hard to photograph from ground
vel but the advent of drones allowed this stunning view to be taken as Southern Railway Class 'S15' No 847 brings its northbound train through the outskirts of East
rinstead in the morning sunshine early in the new year, January 2017. *John Harwood*

East Grinstead station

The locomotives featured on these page bore the brunt of the railway's heaviest trains during the 2019 season, supported by SECR Class 'O1' and 'H' Nos 65 and 263, pictured on pages 24 and 30.

Left: The 'running-in' nameboard, which allows passengers on an arriving train to identify the station, was ready to welcome passengers in September 2010. *Derek Hayward*

Below: **BR CLASS 4 TANK No 80151** returned to service in July 2019 after major overhaul, having been out of service for seven years. It is pictured at East Grinstead with an admiring audience on 5 September 2019. *John Sandys*

Top right: **ARRIVING AT EAST GRINSTEAD** The new station was established ahead of the formal opening in 2013, serving a number of diesel-hauled special trains that ran down to Imberhorne cutting when it was still filled with rubbish. A canopy shelter for passengers was built in 2015 in a traditional style. Here BR Class 5 No 73082 *Camelot* runs slowly to a stand at the north end of the station's single platform on 11 December 2018. *John Sandys*

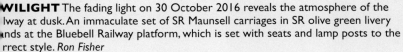

WILIGHT The fading light on 30 October 2016 reveals the atmosphere of the lway at dusk. An immaculate set of SR Maunsell carriages in SR olive green livery nds at the Bluebell Railway platform, which is set with seats and lamp posts to the rrect style. *Ron Fisher*

ft: **SR 'Q' CLASS No 30541** stands at East Grinstead on 25 July 2019. It had been service for four years from its last major repair by the time this picture was taken, but d waited a long time for that repair; its previous period of service had ended in 1993. n *Sandys*

THE END OF THE LINE SR Class 'S15' No 847 moves into the headshunt at East Grinstead on 9 March 2019 to run round its train; the buffer stops beyond mark the very northern extremity of the railway. Just 2 minutes' walk away is the National Rail station, which provides very easy connections with Bluebell services. Beside the locomotive is the water tower, which was constructed in 2014 to provide one of the essentials for any steam locomotive. While most locomotives can carry sufficient coal to make several round trips of the line, smaller locomotives in particular need to take water much more frequently; running out of water can cause major damage to a locomotive. *John Sandys*

Index of Locomotives

BLUEBELL AT 60 The Bluebell Railway began as a sleepy branch line in 1960 but its operations have since become increasingly main-line in character. Longer, heavier trains and larger locomotives now form the mainstay of the service. BR Standard Class 5 *Camelot* exemplifies this as it is pictured near Horsted Keynes on 14 October 2018. *Keith Leppard*